The town is busy today.

Four small wheels go round.
What is it?

It is a blue car. It has got a horn.

Ten big wheels go round.
What is it?

It is a **green** lorry. It has got a loud engine.

vrooooom!

engine

Two thin wheels go round.
What is it?

Ding-a-ling!

It is a **white** bicycle. It has got a nice bell.

Eight fat wheels go round.
What is it?

It is a **yellow** bus.
It has got big wipers.

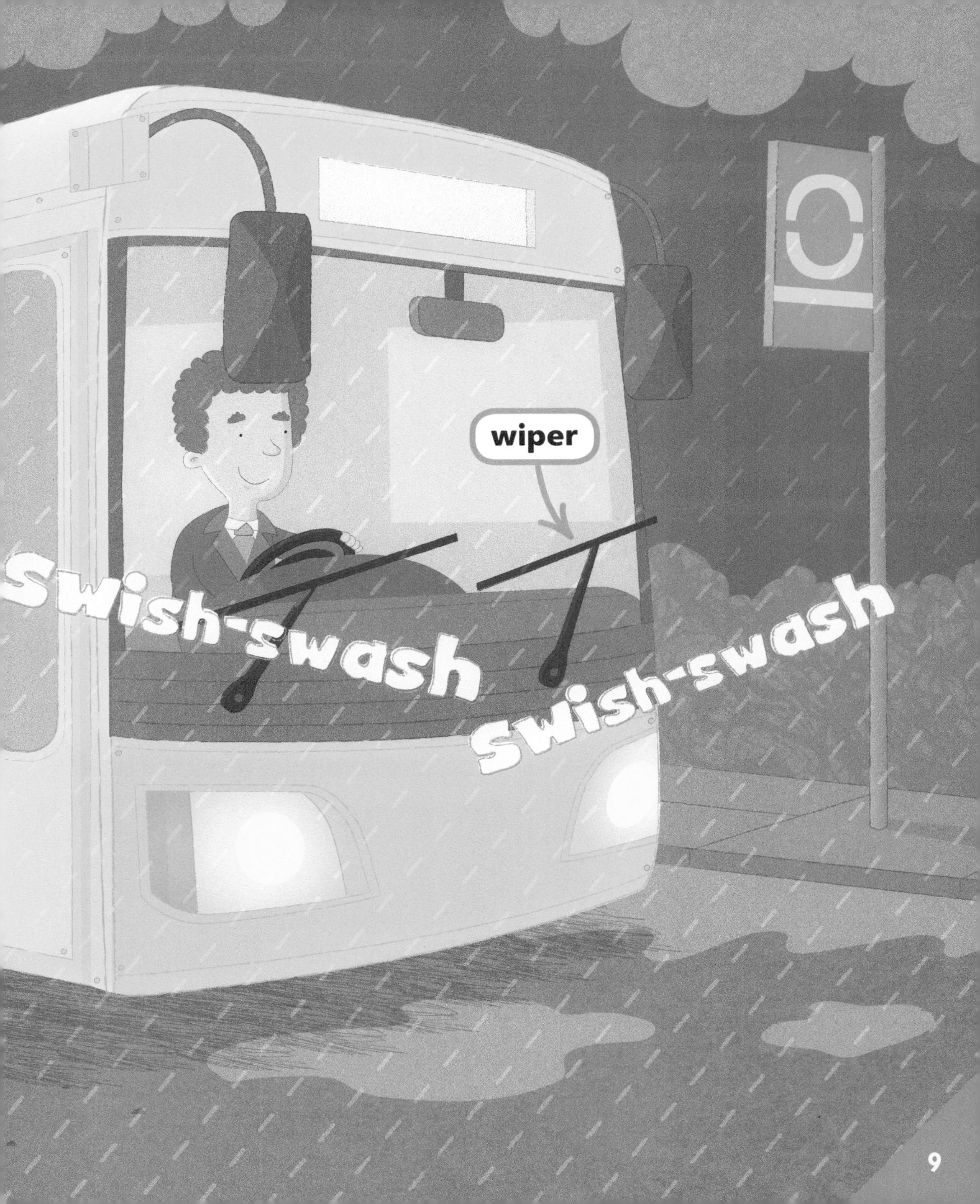
wiper
Swish-swash
Swish-swash

Twelve **black** wheels go round.
What is it?

siren

It is a   fire engine.
It has got a loud siren.

Six big wheels go round.
What is it?

rumble rumble

mixer

It is an orange cement mixer.
The mixer goes round and round.

Activities

Before You Read

1 What do you see on page 1?

After You Read

1 Read and match.

fire engine   bicycle   lorry   car   cement mixer   bus

ⓐ   ⓑ   ⓒ   ⓓ   ⓔ   ⓕ

2 Read and say Yes/No.

a A fire engine has got a siren.

b A bus has got a mixer.

c A car has got a horn.

d A bicycle has got wipers.

e A cement mixer has got ten wheels.

f A lorry has got an engine.

Pearson Education Limited
Edinburgh Gate, Harlow,
Essex CM20 2JE, England
and Associated Companies throughout the world.

ISBN: 978-1-4082-8822-1

This edition first published by Pearson Education Ltd 2013

10

Text copyright © Pearson Education Ltd 2013

The moral rights of the author have been asserted
in accordance with the Copyright Designs and Patents Act 1988

Set in 19/23pt OT Fiendstar
Printed in Great Britain by Ashford Colour Press Ltd.
SWTC/01

Acknowledgements
Illustrations: Mike Byrne (Advocate)

For a complete list of the titles available in the Pearson English Kids Readers series, please go to
www.pearsonenglishkidsreaders.com. Alternatively, write to your local Pearson Education office or to
Pearson English Readers Marketing Department, Pearson Education, Edinburgh Gate, Harlow, Essex CM202JE, England.